The Love Within
By James M.

Dedication

For the girl who taught me love and pain at the same time.

For the boy who gave everything and didn't know how to love yet.

For the man I've become through heartbreak,silence, and fire.

And for anyone who ever lost themselves trying to be enough –
This is where you find yourself again.

Entry 1

Peace in the Chaos

You are my peace in the chaos.

My light through thunder.

My rain when the storms break.

Your voice–my favorite melody.

Entry 2

Away

I love you like the water loves the plant—

Gently, Endlessly, without needing thanks.

But I let you drift away,

Hoping one day...

We'll reconnect.

Entry 3

Unexplained Absence

If i could tell you how i feel,

It wouldn't make sense.

My heart glows in the dark

Every time I hear your name.

And when I'm near you...

It's like the world softens,

And I forget everything but

Your presence.

Entry 4

Living Without

I don't know how to love you—

but I do.

I don't know how to speak without talking,

But somehow,

I know how to tell you how I feel

In this verse.

Entry 5

Waiting

Waiting on you

Like flowers wait for spring.

One touch from you–

And I come undone.

Still holding my breath

For something you may never say

Gripping the last thread

Of what we used to be.

Entry 6

One Last Time

Your smile lights up the world.

Your laugh–

My favorite song,

One I'll sing until the end of time.

Still hoping

To hold your hand

One last time.

Entry 7

Fixing Love

Trying to fix what I've broken...

But is it working?

I don't know.

The silence is killing me—

I'm so full of love,

I feel like I'm about to burst.

But I don't know how to give it

Without losing myself.

Entry 8

Unspoken Tears

I want to cry

But I have no more tears.

I want to come to you,

But I have no way to make it.

Even though we're

A thousand miles apart,

I'll hold on–

forever.

Entry 9

Memories

Why did I fall in love with you?

I told myself I wouldn't...

But I failed.

Your beauty,

Your laugh,

Your smile–

The way you looked at me

Turned my whole world over.

Entry 10

Ours

I don't know

Where this road is going to lead

Between us.

But i'm gonna fight

To keep it alive–

Every memory,

Every argument,

Every quiet night–

They're ours.

And I'll carry them with me

No matter where we end up.

Entry 11

Delusion

I tried to tell myself

I wasn't falling in love.

But it was only a delusion—

Playing tricks on me like Halloween.

No costume, no disguise,

Just me...

And this love.

No treats—

Just the truth I kept trying to hide.

Entry 12

Holding on

I poured my heart out–

Now I'm nervous

And lost.

Waiting on a response,

Checking every minute,

Realizing...

It may never come.

Entry 13

The War

Trying to let go,

But the memories

Keep rushing back–

Attacking my soul.

I'm fighting them off,

But I don't know

If I should let go...

Or fight back.

I'm tired.

So tired.

Entry 14

Sacrifice

I gave you everything

My heart had to offer.

Now i'm sitting

In silence.

I've begged.

I've cried.

I've stopped moving

Just to feel the weight of it.

But now...

I must move–

For your love,

Even if it's not mine to hold.

Entry 15

You Said

You told me

You'd never leave me–

But you did.

You told me

You loved me–

But still,

You left.

How can I trust you...

And yet,

I still love you.

Entry 16

Sleepless

Laying in bed

Twisting and turning

Like a tornado–

Thinking of you.

I can't sleep.

My mind racing,

Searching for a way

To get you back

In my arms.

But I don't know...

If you even feel the same.

Entry 17

Echoes

I'm trying to distract myself–

But it's not working.

Your voice keeps echoing

Over and over

In my mind.

I keep replaying what we had,

Trying to be strong–

But inside...

I'm weak.

How do I move forward

Without you?

Entry 18

Facing Pain

I'm tired

Of running from what I feel.

But I don't have the words

To say it out loud.

So I write...

Hoping to release it.

But sometimes

The more I write,

The harder it gets

To let go.

Entry 19

The Door

I keep checking my phone

to see if you responded.

Guess not.

And I wonder...

What are you feeling?

Do you still love?

Or are you afraid

to open the door?

Entry 20

Regret

If I could do it all over again...

I'd treat you differently.

I would've respected

Who you are–

All of you.

But I can't go back in time.

So now...

I live with the regret.

Entry 21

Afraid

How we met

Was rare.

I still think about how it even

Happened.

But now...

I'm afraid to take the next step.

I tell myself I'm ready–

But the truth is

I'm not.

Entry 22

Mistaken Hope

My heart dropped.

I thought I got a text from you—

but it was someone else.

Now my chest is pounding,

scared,

because for a moment

I thought

I had you back.

Entry 23

Confusion

As if it's really over

Between us?

I can't let it end

Without a fight.

I can't give up

On loving you–

Not yet.

I didn't have you

For long...

So what must I do

Now?

Entry 24

I'm Sorry

I hurt you deeply–

And I'm sorry.

I made you cry...

And it broke my spirit.

Everything went dark.

Completely.

And then you left.

And now,

I can't forgive myself

For what I've done

To you.

I'm

Sorry.

Entry 25

Dead Heart

She finally responded.

And now I know–

It's over.

For real.

She said everything...

And I can't move.

My kryptonite?

It was hope.

And now my heart...

Is dead.

Last

You told me everything I needed

to hear, but didn't want to.

I did you wrong–

And now you're gone.

Now I sit in the dark,

Tears sliding down a face that once

smiled for you.

My chest?

Feels like it's folding inward.

My mind?

Replays your goodbye like a song on loop.

You were my light,

and now my world has evaporated

into silence.

And all I can do now...

Is ache in the space where you

used to live.

Entry 27

Nightmare

I keep hoping this is a dream,

that I'll open my eyes...

and you'll be there beside me,

peaceful,

real,

ours.

But the truth sinks in deeper

Every second.

This isn't a dream...

It's a nightmare–

one I didn't choose,

one I don't want to face.

I keep reaching for you

in my sleep,

but you're just air.

And when I wake up

I'm still alone.

Still broken.

Still whispering your name to an empty room.

Entry 28

Home

I wish you'd give me

another chance.

Just one.

Let go of pride—

or fear,

or the guilt that keeps you

from looking me in the eyes.

I wish you'd come back home.

Not just to me—

but to us.

But deep down

I know you won't.

And now I'm just here—

staring at the door,

wondering what I could've done

differently, wishing I could hold

your hand, knowing I never will again.

I still call this place home...

but without you,it's just walls.

Unseen

When we were talking

I shed tears–

but didn't let them fall.

I was afraid you'd see me as weak.

Now you'll never see me again.

And you'll never know...

that was the hardest goodbye

I ever held in.

Entry 30

Letting Go

I love you.

More than I ever showed,

more than i could ever say.

I didn't want you to leave–

I begged in silence.

Prayed in pain.

But I love you enough

to let you go.

Not because I stopped caring

but because I finally realized–

Loving someone doesn't always

mean holding on.

Sometimes it means standing still

while they walk away

and whispering to yourself:

"I'll guard the love, even if I lose the person."

Entry 31

The Change

I finally got up after weeping...

and looked at myself.

Not the broken man.

Not the one she left behind.

But the fighter.

The one still standing.

And I said to myself–

"This is who I am.

I've changed!!"

Entry 32

The Lesson

Love taught me more while

I was losing it

than while I was holding on.

I learned that actions speak louder

than words.

And that you can love someone

with your whole soul...

and still lose them.

The lesson?

I won't hold back next time.

I'll give love fully–

Not with fear

But with truth.

Entry 33

The Fire

She left me...

but the fire in me didn't

The pain

the regret

that's my fuel now.

And I own it,

not for her–

but for me.

For everything I'm becoming.

Entry 34

The Apology

I'm sorry

not to her

but to myself

for the times I didn't know how to love

the times I froze when I

should've pulled closer for

being afraid

I was learning

I was living

I didn't know better

but now, I do.

And I forgive that version of me

because he still showed up.

And without him

I wouldn't be the man writing

this now.

Entry 35

The Take

I used to write from heartbreak.

Now I write from peace.

The tears still flow...

but they don't drown me anymore.

I still remember her

but I remember me more.

That's the take.

When love no longer defines you,

You define yourself.

And now?

Every word I write is for

the man i'm becoming.

Entry 36

Vision

I'm not chasing love anymore–

I'm building something deeper.

A legacy

A purpose

A future only I can see

"Every bruise, every scar,"

Every silent night taught me this:

I was never meant to stay broken.

I was meant to become unbreakable.

And the man I'm becoming

He doesn't beg.

He doesn't wait

He builds.

And when the right one comes

She'll walk beside me–

Not in front, not behind.

Entry 37

The Woman Who Stayed

You didn't meet the broken me—

you met the man I became

After the storm.

You saw my scars

And stayed.

Not because it was easy,

but because love, to you,

meant holding on.

And now everything I build...

Has a place for you in it.

Entry 38

Goodbye

I don't hate you

I never could

You were part of my story

I'll never forget.

I loved you hard

I lost myself trying to hold on.

But this isn't pain anymore–

it's peace.

This is me letting go

not because I stopped

loving you...

but because I finally

started loving myself.

Goodbye.

And thank you–

For the lesson, for the love ,

For the growth.

Entry 39

The Return

I gave everything to love...

and lost parts of me along the way.

But now I'm back.

Not broken–

Just rebuilt.

I look in the mirror

and this time I don't see pain.

I see me.

Entry 40

The Love Within

I thought love would save me.

I thought if I gave everything–

someone would stay.

But I gave, and I gave,

until I had nothing left but silence.

And in that silence...

I found something I didn't expect.

Me.

Not the strong version I showed the world–

but the broken boy inside

who just wanted to be seen.

I sat with him

I wept with him

And i forgave him–

for all the things he didn't know.

For loving too fast.

For hurting others while trying to heal.

For searching for safety in people who weren't

safe.

I told him:

"You don't need to be fixed.

You need to be loved–by you."

And that's when I stopped

Looking outward.

That's when I came home.

I used to think love was something

I had to earn.

Now I know–

The rarest kind of love...

is the kind you fight to find within.

And I found it

through the pain

through the fire

through the silence.

I found me.